Former congressional staffers reveal best practices for **making Congress listen**

INDIVISIBLE:
A PRACTICAL GUIDE for RESISTING THE TRUMP AGENDA

NOTE FROM THE INDIVISIBLE TEAM

Since this guide went live as a Google Doc, we've received an overwhelming flood of messages from people all over the country working to resist the Trump agenda. We're thrilled and humbled by the energy and passion of this growing movement. We'll be updating the guide based on your feedback and making it interactive ASAP. You can sign up for updates at www.IndivisibleGuide.com.

Every single person who worked on this guide and website is a volunteer. We're doing this in our free time without coordination or support from our employers. Our only goal is to help the real leaders on the ground who are resisting Trump's agenda on their home turf. We hope you will take this document and use it however you see fit.

We want to hear your stories, questions, comments, edits, etc., so please feel free to ping some of us on Twitter: @IndivisibleTeam, @ezralevin, @angelrafpadilla, @texpat, @Leahgreenb. Or email IndivisibleAgainstTrump@gmail.com.

And please please please spread the word! Only folks who know this exists will use it.

Good luck - we will win.

NOTE TO IMMIGRANTS AND NONCITIZENS

The U.S. Constitution ensures equal representation for all individuals living in the United States, regardless of income, race, ethnicity, gender, sexual orientation, age, or immigration status. Noncitizens, though they may lack the right to vote in federal elections, have the right to have their voices heard by their representatives in Congress.

This guide is intended to serve as a resource to all individuals who would like to more effectively participate in the democratic process. While we encourage noncitizens to participate to the extent that they are able, individuals should only take actions that they are comfortable taking, and should consider their particular set of circumstances before engaging in any of these activities.

Individuals are under no obligation to provide any personally identifiable information to a member of Congress or their staff. Individuals may be asked for their name and zip code, but this is only to confirm that the person is a constituent, and providing this information is strictly voluntarily. NO ONE is required to provide any additional information, such as address, social

Updated by the Indivisible Team on January 5, 2017.

Indivisible: A Practical Guide for Resisting the Trump Agenda is licensed under the Creative Commons Attribution-NonCommercial-ShareAlike 4.0 International License. To view a copy of this license, visit http://creativecommons.org/licenses/by-nc-sa/4.0/.

A Partial List of Contributors to the Indivisible Guide:
Angel Padilla, Billy Fleming, Caroline Kavit, Ezra Levin, Gonzalo Martinez de Vedia, Indivar Dutta-Gupta, Jennay Ghowrwal, Jeremy Haile, Leah Greenberg, Mary Humphreys, Matt Traldi, Sara Clough, and Sarah Dohl.

INTRODUCTION

Donald Trump is the biggest popular vote loser in history to ever call himself President-Elect. In spite of the fact that he has no mandate, he will attempt to use his congressional majority to reshape America in his own racist, authoritarian, and corrupt image. If progressives are going to stop this, we must stand indivisibly opposed to Trump and the members of Congress (MoCs) who would do his bidding. **Together, we have the power to resist — and we have the power to win.**

We know this because we've seen it before. The authors of this guide are former congressional staffers who witnessed the rise of the Tea Party. We saw these activists take on a popular president with a mandate for change and a supermajority in Congress. We saw them organize locally and convince their own MoCs to reject President Obama's agenda. Their ideas were wrong, cruel, and tinged with racism — and they won.

We believe that protecting our values, our neighbors, and ourselves will require mounting a similar resistance to the Trump agenda — but a resistance built on the values of inclusion, tolerance, and fairness. Trump is not popular. He does not have a mandate. He does not have large congressional majorities. If a small minority in the Tea Party can stop President Obama, then we the majority can stop a petty tyrant named Trump.

WHO IS THIS DOCUMENT BY AND FOR?

We: Are former progressive congressional staffers who saw the Tea Party beat back President Obama's agenda.

We: See the enthusiasm to fight the Trump agenda and want to share insider info on how best to influence Congress to do that.

You: Want to do your part to beat back the Trump agenda and understand that will require more than calls and petitions.

You: Should use this guide, share it, amend it, make it your own, and get to work.

To this end, the following chapters offer a step-by-step guide for individuals, groups, and organizations looking to replicate the Tea Party's success in getting Congress to listen to a small, vocal, dedicated group of constituents. The guide is intended to be equally useful for stiffening Democratic spines and weakening pro-Trump Republican resolve.

We believe that the next four years depend on Americans across the country standing indivisible against the Trump agenda. We believe that buying into false promises or accepting partial concessions will only further empower Trump to victimize us and our neighbors. We hope that this guide will provide those who share that belief useful tools to make Congress listen.

ONE PAGE SUMMARY

Here's the quick and dirty summary of this document. While this page summarizes top-level takeaways, the full document describes how to actually carry out these activities.

CHAPTER 1
How grassroots advocacy worked to stop President Obama. We examine lessons from the Tea Party's rise and recommend two key strategic components:

1. A local strategy targeting individual Members of Congress (MoCs).
2. A defensive approach purely focused on stopping Trump from implementing an agenda built on racism, authoritarianism, and corruption.

CHAPTER 2
How your MoC thinks — reelection, reelection, reelection — and how to use that to save democracy. MoCs want their constituents to think well of them and they want good, local press. They hate surprises, wasted time, and most of all, bad press that makes them look weak, unlikable, and vulnerable. You will use these interests to make them listen and act.

CHAPTER 3
Identify or organize your local group. Is there an existing local group or network you can join? Or do you need to start your own? We suggest steps to help mobilize your fellow constituents locally and start organizing for action.

CHAPTER 4
Four local advocacy tactics that actually work. Most of you have three MoCs — two Senators and one Representative. Whether you like it or not, they are your voices in Washington. Your job is to make sure they are, in fact, speaking for you. We've identified four key opportunity areas that just a handful of local constituents can use to great effect. Always record encounters on video, prepare questions ahead of time, coordinate with your group, and report back to local media:

1. **Town halls.** MoCs regularly hold public in-district events to show that they are listening to constituents. Make them listen to you, and report out when they don't.
2. **Non-town hall events.** MoCs love cutting ribbons and kissing babies back home. Don't let them get photo-ops without questions about racism, authoritarianism, and corruption.
3. **District office sit-ins/meetings.** Every MoC has one or several district offices. Go there. Demand a meeting with the MoC. Report to the world if they refuse to listen.
4. **Coordinated calls.** Calls are a light lift but can have an impact. Organize your local group to barrage your MoCs at an opportune moment about and on a specific issue.

CHAPTER 1: HOW GRASSROOTS ADVOCACY WORKED TO STOP PRESIDENT OBAMA

"If they succeed, or even half succeed, the Tea Party's most important legacy may be organizational, not political."
— Jonathan Rauch

Like us, you probably deeply disagree with the principles and positions of the Tea Party. But we can all learn from their success in influencing the national debate and the behavior of national policymakers. To their credit, they thought thoroughly about advocacy tactics, as the leaked "Town Hall Action Memo" demonstrates.

This chapter draws on both research and our own experiences as former congressional staffers to illustrate the strengths of the Tea Party movement and to provide lessons to leverage in the fight against Trump's racism, authoritarianism, and corruption.

THE TEA PARTY'S TWO KEY STRATEGIC CHOICES

The Tea Party's success came down to two critical strategic elements:

1. They were locally focused. The Tea Party started as an organic movement built on small local groups of dedicated conservatives. Yes, they received some support/coordination from above, but fundamentally all the hubbub was caused by a relatively small number of conservatives working together.

» Groups started as disaffected conservatives talking to each other online. In response to the 2008 bank bailouts and President Obama's election, groups began forming to discuss their anger and what could be done. They eventually realized that the locally-based discussion groups themselves could be a powerful tool.

» Groups were small, local, and dedicated. Tea Party groups could be fewer than 10 people, but they were highly localized and dedicated significant personal time and resources. Members communicated with each other regularly, tracked developments in Washington, and coordinated advocacy efforts together.

» Groups were relatively few in number. The Tea Party was not hundreds of thousands of people spending every waking hour focused on advocacy. Rather, the efforts were somewhat modest. Only 1 in 5 self-identified Tea Partiers contributed money or attended events. On any given day in 2009 or 2010, only twenty local events — meetings, trainings, town halls, etc. — were scheduled nationwide. In short, a relatively small number of groups were having a big impact on the national debate.

WHAT THE TEA PARTY ACCOMPLISHED

The Tea Party organized to end hope for progressive reform under President Obama. Their members:

- Changed votes and defeated legislation
- Radically slowed federal policymaking
- Forced Republicans to reject compromise
- Shaped national debate over President Obama's agenda
- Paved the way for the Republican takeover in 2010 and Donald Trump today

These were real, tangible results by a group that represented only a small portion of Americans.

THE TEA PARTY'S IDEAS WERE WRONG

The Tea Party's ideas were wrong, and their behavior was often horrible. Their members:

- Ignored reality and made up their own facts
- Threatened anyone they considered an enemy
- Physically assaulted and spat on staff
- Shouted obscenities and burned people in effigy
- Targeted their hate not just at Congress, but also fellow citizens (especially people of color)

We are better than this. We are the majority, and we don't need petty scare tactics to win.

2. They were almost purely defensive. The Tea Party focused on saying NO to Members of Congress (MoCs) on their home turf. While the Tea Party activists were united by a core set of shared beliefs, they actively avoided developing their own policy agenda. Instead, they had an extraordinary clarity of purpose, united in opposition to President Obama. They didn't accept concessions and treated weak Republicans as traitors.

> Groups focused on defense, not policy development. In response to the 2008 bank bailouts and President Obama's election, groups began forming to discuss their anger and what could be done. They eventually realized that the locally-based discussion groups themselves could be a powerful tool.

> Groups rejected concessions to Democrats and targeted weak Republicans. Tea Partiers viewed concessions to Democrats as betrayal. This limited their ability to negotiate, but they didn't care. Instead they focused on scaring congressional Democrats and keeping Republicans honest. As a result, few Republicans spoke against the Tea Party for fear of attracting blowback.

> Groups focused on local congressional representation. Tea Partiers primarily applied this defensive strategy by pressuring their own local MoCs. This meant demanding that their Representatives and Senators be their voice of opposition on Capitol Hill. At a tactical level, the Tea Party had several replicable practices, including:

> Showing up to the MoC's town hall meetings and demanding answers

> Showing up to the MoC's office and demanding a meeting

> Coordinating blanket calling of congressional offices at key moments

USING THESE LESSONS TO FIGHT THE TRUMP AGENDA

For the next two years, Donald Trump and congressional Republicans will control the federal government. But they will depend on just about every MoC to actually get laws passed. And those MoC care much more about getting reelected than they care about any specific issue. By adopting a defensive strategy that pressures MoCs, we can achieve the following goals:

» Stall the Trump agenda by forcing them to redirect energy away from their priorities. Congressional offices have limited time and limited people. A day that they spend worrying about you is a day that they're not ending Medicare, privatizing public schools, or preparing a Muslim registry.

» Sap Representatives' will to support or drive reactionary change. If you do this right, you will have an outsized impact. Every time your MoC signs on to a bill, takes a position, or makes a statement, a little part of his or her mind will be thinking: "How am I going to explain this to the angry constituents who keep showing up at my events and demanding answers?"

» Reaffirm the illegitimacy of the Trump agenda. The hard truth is that Trump, McConnell, and Ryan will have the votes to cause some damage. But by objecting as loudly and powerfully as possible, and by centering the voices of those who are most affected by their agenda, you can ensure that people understand exactly how bad these laws are from the very start – priming the ground for the 2018 midterms and their repeal when Democrats

SHOULDN'T WE PUT FORWARD AN ALTERNATE, POSITIVE AGENDA?

A defensive strategy does not mean dropping your own policy priorities or staying silent on an alternate vision for our country over the next four years. What it means is that, when you're trying to influence your MoC, you will have the most leverage when you are focused on whatever the current legislative priority is.

You may not like the idea of being purely defensive; we certainly don't. As progressives, our natural inclination is to talk about the things we're for — a clean climate, economic justice, health care for all, racial equality, gender and sexual equality, and peace and human rights. These are the things that move us. But the hard truth of the next four years is that we're not going to set the agenda; Trump and congressional Republicans will, and we'll have to respond. The best way to stand up for the progressive values and policies we cherish is to stand together, indivisible — to treat an attack on one as an attack on all.

retake power.

CHAPTER 2: HOW YOUR MEMBER OF CONGRESS THINKS, AND HOW TO USE THAT TO SAVE DEMOCRACY

"There go the people. I must follow them, for I am their leader."
— Alexandre Ledru-Rollin

This chapter explains how congressional offices and the people within them work, and what that means for your advocacy strategy.

IT'S ALL ABOUT REELECTION, REELECTION, REELECTION

To influence your own Member of Congress (MoC), you have to understand one thing: every House member runs for office every two years and every Senator runs for election every six years. Functionally speaking, MoCs are always either running for office or getting ready for their next election — a fact that shapes everything they do.

To be clear, this does not mean that your MoC is cynical and unprincipled. The vast majority of people in Congress believe in their ideals, and care deeply about representing their constituents and having a positive impact. But they also know that if they want to make change, they need to stay in office.

This constant reelection pressure means that MoCs are enormously sensitive to their image in the district or state, and will work very hard to avoid signs of public dissent or disapproval. What every MoC wants — regardless of party — is for his or her constituents to agree with the following narrative:

"My MoC cares about me, shares my values, and is working hard for me."

— *What every MoC wants their constituents to think.*

HELP, MY MEMBER OF CONGRESS IS IN A SAFE DISTRICT

If your actions threaten this narrative, then you will unnerve your MoC and change their decision-making process. If your MoC is in a heavily Democratic or Republican district, you may assume that they have a safe seat and there's nothing you can do to influence them. This is not true! The reality is that no MoC ever considers themselves to be safe from all threats. MoCs who have nothing to fear from a general election still worry about primary challenges.

More broadly, no one stays an MoC without being borderline compulsive about protecting their image. Even the safest MoC will be deeply alarmed by signs of organized opposition, because these actions create the impression that they're not connected to their district and not listening to their constituents.

HELP, MY MOCS ARE ACTUALLY PRETTY GOOD!

Congratulations! Your Senators and Representative are doing what they should to fight racism, authoritarianism, and corruption. They're making the right public statements, co-sponsoring the right bills, and voting the right way. So how does this change your strategy? Two key things to keep in mind:

Do NOT switch to targeting other MoCs who don't represent you. They don't represent you, and they don't care what you have to say. Stick with your own local MoCs.

DO use this guide to engage with your MoCs locally. Instead of pressuring them to do the right thing, praise them for doing the right thing. This is important because it will help ensure that they continue to do the right thing. Congressional staff are rarely contacted when the MoC does something good — your efforts locally will provide highly valuable positive reinforcement.

WHAT DOES A MOC'S OFFICE DO, AND WHY?

A MoC's office is composed of roughly 15-25 staff for House offices and 60-70 for Senate offices, spread across a D.C. and one or several district offices. MoC offices perform the following functions:

- » **Constituent services.** Staff connect with both individual constituents and local organizations, serving as a link to and an advocate within the federal government on issues such as visas, grant applications, and public benefits.

- » **Communicate with constituents directly.** Staff take calls, track constituent messages, and write letters to stay in touch with constituents' priorities, follow up on specific policy issues that constituents have expressed concern about, and reinforce the message that they are listening.

- » **Meet with constituents.** MoCs and staff meet with constituents to learn about local priorities and build connections.

- » **Seek and create positive press.** Staff try to shape press coverage and public information to create a favorable image for the MoC.

- » **Host and attend events in district.** Representatives host and attend events in the district to connect with constituents, understand their priorities, and get good local press.

- » **Actual legislating.** MoCs and staff decide their policy positions, develop and sponsor bills, and take votes based on a combination of their own beliefs, pressure from leadership/lobbyists, and pressure from their constituents.

WHAT YOUR MOC CARES ABOUT

When it comes to constituent interactions, MoCs care about things that make them look good, responsive, and hardworking to the people of their district. In practice, that means that they care about some things very much, and other things very little:

YOUR MOC CARES A LOT ABOUT	YOUR MOC DOESN'T CARE MUCH ABOUT
Verified constituents from the district (or state for Senators)	People from outside the district (or state for Senators)
Advocacy that requires effort — the more effort, the more they care. Calls, personal emails, and especially showing up in person in the district	Form letters, a Tweet, or Facebook comment (unless they generate widespread attention)
Local press and editorials, maybe national press	Wonky D.C.-based news (depends on the MoC)
An interest group's endorsement	Your thoughtful analysis of the proposed bill
Groups of constituents, locally famous individuals, or big individual campaign contributors	A single constituent
Concrete asks that entail a verifiable action — vote for a bill, make a public statement, etc.	General ideas about the world
A single ask in your communication — letter, email, phone call, office visit, etc.	A laundry list of all the issues you're concerned about

WHAT YOUR MOC IS THINKING: GOOD OUTCOME VS. BAD OUTCOME

To make this a bit more concrete and show where advocacy comes in, below are some examples of actions that a MoC might take, what they're hoping to see happen as a result, and what they really don't want to see happen. Some MoCs will go to great lengths to avoid bad outcomes —

EXAMPLE ACTION	DESIRED OUTCOME	BAD OUTCOME
Letter to Constituent	Constituent feels happy that their concerns were answered.	Constituent posts letter on social media saying it didn't answer their questions or didn't answer for weeks/months, calls Congressman Bob unresponsive and untrustworthy.
In-district Event	Local newspaper reports that Congresswoman Sara appeared at opening of new bridge, which she helped secure funding for.	Local newspaper reports that protestors barraged Congresswoman Sara with questions about corruption in the infrastructure bill.
Town Hall / Listening Session	Local newspaper reports that Congressman Bob hosted a town hall and discussed his work to balance the budget.	Local newspaper reports that angry constituents strongly objected to Congressman Bob's support for privatizing Medicare.
Policy Position	Congresswoman Sara votes on a bill and releases a press statement hailing it as a step forward.	Congresswoman Sara's phones are deluged with calls objecting to the bill. A group of constituents stage an event outside her district office and invite press to hear them talk about how the bill will personally hurt their families.

even as far as changing their positions or public statements.

CHAPTER 3: ORGANIZE A LOCAL GROUP TO FIGHT FOR YOUR CONGRESSIONAL DISTRICT

> *"We need in every bay and community a group of angelic troublemakers."*
> – Bayard Rustin

The Tea Party formed organically as conservatives upset after the 2008 election came together in local discussion groups. We believe the same thing is happening now across the country as progressives — in person, in already existing networks, and on Facebook — come together to move forward. The big question for these groups is: what's next?

If you're reading this, you're probably already part of a local network of people who want to stop the Trump agenda — even if it's just your friends or a group on Facebook. This chapter is about how to take that energy to the next level, and start fighting locally to take the country back.

SHOULD I FORM A GROUP?

There's no need to reinvent the wheel — if an activist group or network is already attempting to do congressional advocacy along these lines, just join up with them. Depending on your Representative's district, it may make sense to have more than one group. This congressional map tool (https://www.govtrack.us/congress/members/map) shows the boundaries for your district.

If you look around and can't find a group working specifically on local action focused on your Members of Congress (MoCs) in your area, just start doing it! It's not rocket science. You really just need two things:

» Ten or so people (but even fewer is a fine start!) who are geographically nearby — ideally in the same congressional district

» A commitment from those people to devote a couple hours per month to fighting the

DIVERSITY IN YOUR GROUP & REACHING OUT

Trump's agenda explicitly targets immigrants, Muslims, people of color, LGBTQ people, the poor and working class, and women. It is critical that our resistance reflect and center the voices of those who are most directly threatened by the Trump agenda. If you are forming a group, we urge you to make a conscious effort to pursue diversity and solidarity at every stage in the process. Being inclusive and diverse might include recruiting members who can bridge language gaps, and finding ways to accommodate participation when people can't attend due to work schedules, health issues, or childcare needs.

In addition, where there are local groups already organizing around the rights of those most threatened by the Trump agenda, we urge you to reach out to partner with them, amplify their voices, and defer to their leadership.

racism, authoritarianism, and corruption pushed by Trump

HOW TO FORM A GROUP

If you do want to form a group, here are our recommendations on how to go about it:

1. **Decide you're going to start a local group** dedicated to making your MoCs aware of their constituents' opposition to the Trump agenda. This might be a subgroup of an already existing activist group, or it might be a new effort — it really depends on your circumstances. Start where people are: if you're in a group with a lot of people who want to do this kind of thing, then start there; if you're not, you'll need to find them somewhere else. The most important thing is that this is a LOCAL group. Your band of heroes is focused on applying local pressure, which means you all need to be local.

2. **Identify a few additional co-founders** who are interested in participating and recruiting others. Ideally, these are people who have different social networks from you so that you can maximize your reach. Make an effort to ensure that leadership of the group reflects the diversity of opposition to Trump.

3. **Email your contacts and post a message on your Facebook**, on any local Facebook groups that you're a member of, and/or other social media channels you use regularly. Say that you're starting a group for constituents of Congresswoman Sara,

HOW DO I RECRUIT PEOPLE TO TAKE ACTION?

Most people are moved to take action through individual conversations. Here are some tips for having successful conversations to inspire people to take action with your group.

1. **Get the story.** What issues does the other person care about? How would the reactionary Republican agenda affect them, their communities, and their values?

2. **Imagine what's possible.** How can your group change your community's relationship with your MoC? How could your group, and others like it, protect our values?

3. **Commitment and ownership.** Ask a clear yes or no question: will you work with me to hold our representatives accountable? Then, get to specifics. Who else can they talk to about joining the group? What work needs to be done — planning a meeting, researching a MoC — that they can take on? When will you follow up?

Ask open-ended questions! People are more likely to take action when they articulate what they care about and can connect it to the action they are going to take. A good rule of thumb is to talk 30% of the time or less and listen at least 70% of the time.

dedicated to stopping the Trump agenda, and ask people to email you to sign up.

4. **Invite everyone who has expressed interest to an in-person kickoff meeting.** Use this meeting to agree on a name, principles for your group, roles for leadership, a way of communicating, and a strategy for your MoC. Rule of thumb: 50% of the people who have said they are definitely coming will show up to your meeting. Aim high! Get people to commit to come — they'll want to because saving democracy is fun.

    » **Manage the meeting:** Keep people focused on the ultimate core strategy: applying pressure to your MoC to stop Trump. Other attendees may have other ideas — or may be coming to share their concerns about Trump — and it's important to affirm their concerns and feelings. But it's also important to redirect that energy and make sure that the conversation stays focused on developing a group and a plan of action dedicated to this strategy.

    » **Decide on a name:** Good names include the geographic area of your group, so that it's clear that you're rooted in the community — e.g., "Springfield Indivisible Against Hate." You are 100% welcome to pick up and run with the Indivisible name if you want, but we won't be hurt if you don't.

    » **Agree on principles:** This is your chance to say what your group stands for. We recommend two guiding principles:

    » Donald Trump's agenda will take America backwards and must be stopped.

    » In order to work together to achieve this goal, we must model the values of inclusion, tolerance, and fairness.

    > As discussed in the second chapter, we strongly recommend focusing on defense against the Trump agenda rather than developing an entire alternative policy agenda. Defining a proactive agenda is time-intensive, divisive, and, quite frankly, a distraction, since there is zero chance that we as progressives will get to put our agenda into action at the federal level in the next four years.

    » **Volunteer for roles:** Figure out how to divide roles and responsibilities among your group. This can look very different depending on who's in the room, but at a minimum, you probably want 1-2 people in charge of overall group coordination, a designated media/social media contact, and 1-2 people in charge of tracking the congressional office's schedule and events. In addition to these administrative roles, ask attendees how they want to contribute to advocacy efforts: attend events, record events, ask questions, make calls, host meetings, engage on social media, write op-eds for local papers, etc.

    » **Adopt means of communication:** You need a way of reaching everyone in your group in order to coordinate actions. This can be a Facebook group, a Google group, a Slack team — whatever people are most comfortable with. It may be wise to consider secure or encrypted platforms such as Signal and WhatsApp.

5. **Expand!** Enlist your members to recruit across their networks. Ask every member to send out the same outreach emails/posts that you did.

» Recruit people for your email list — 100 or 200 isn't unreasonable.

» We strongly recommend making a conscious effort to diversify your group and particularly to center around and defer to communities of people who are most directly affected by the Trump administration's racism, xenophobia, transphobia, homophobia, and antipathy towards the poor. This could include both reaching out through your own networks and forming relationships with community groups that are already working on protecting the rights of marginalized groups.

ALREADY HAVE A GROUP?

Sign up at www.indivisibleguide.com. We're creating a public directory of groups to help you make connections on your home turf. We'll also be sending special updates to group leaders to help build local congressional action plans.

Your group may be pursuing the Indivisible strategy as your main goal or as part of a broader mission. Whatever works!

CHAPTER 4: FOUR LOCAL ADVOCACY TACTICS THAT ACTUALLY WORK

" Every moment is an organizing opportunity, every person a potential activist, every minute a chance to change the world."
— Dolores Huerta

This chapter describes the nuts and bolts of implementing four advocacy tactics to put pressure on your three Members of Congress (MoCs) — your Representative and two Senators. Before we get there though, there's a few things all local groups should do:

Begin with these five steps to gather intel. Before anything else, take the following five steps to arm yourself with information necessary for all future advocacy activities.

1. Find your three MoCs, their official websites, and their office contact info at www.callmycongress.com.

2. Sign up on your MoCs' website to receive regular email updates, invites to local events, and propaganda to understand what they're saying. Every MoC has an e-newsletter.

3. Find out where your MoCs stands on the issues of the day — appointment of white supremacists, tax cuts for the rich, etc. Review their voting history at VoteSmart.org. Research their biggest campaign contributors at OpenSecrets.org.

4. Set up a Google News Alert (http://www.google.com/alerts) — for example for "Rep. Bob Smith" — to receive an email whenever your MoC is in the news.

5. Research on Google News (https://news.google.com/news) what local reporters have written about your MoCs. Find and follow them on Twitter, and build relationships. Before you attend or plan an event, reach out and explain why your group is protesting and provide them background materials and a quote. Journalists on deadline — even those who might not agree with you — appreciate when you provide easy material for a

NOTE ON SAFETY AND PRIVILEGE

We do not yet know how Trump supporters will respond to organized shows of opposition, but we have seen enough to be very concerned that minorities will be targeted or singled out. Plan your actions to ensure that no one is asked to take on a role that they are not comfortable with — especially those roles that call for semi-confrontational behavior — and be mindful of the fact that not everyone is facing an equal level of threat. Members of your group who enjoy more privilege should think carefully about how they can ensure that they are using their privilege to support other members of the group. If you are concerned about potential law enforcement intimidation, consider downloading your state's version of the ACLU Mobile Justice app to ensure that any intimidating behavior is captured on film.

story.

OPPORTUNITY 1
TOWN HALLS/LISTENING SESSIONS

MoCs regularly hold local "Town Halls" or public listening sessions throughout their districts or state. Tea Partiers used these events to great effect — both to directly pressure their MoCs and to attract media to their cause.

PREPARATION

1. **Find out when your MoC's next public town hall event is.** Sometimes these are announced well in advance, and sometimes they are "public" but only sent to select constituents through mailings shortly before the event. If you can't find announcements online, call your MoC directly to find out. When you call, be friendly and say to the staffer, "Hi, I'm a constituent, and I'd like to know when his/her next town hall forum will be." If they don't know, ask to be added to the email list so that you get notified when they do.

2. **Send out a notice of the town hall to your group and get commitments from members to attend.** Distribute to all of them whatever information you have on your MoC's voting record, as well as the prepared questions.

3. **Prepare several questions ahead of time for your group to ask.** Your questions should be sharp and fact-based, ideally including information on the MoC's record, votes they've taken, or statements they've made. Thematically, they should focus on a limited number of issues to maximize impact. Prepare 5-10 of these questions and hand them out to your group ahead of the meeting. Example question:

   "I and many district families in Springfield rely on Medicare. I don't think we should be rationing health care for seniors, and the plan to privatize Medicare will create serious financial hardship for seniors who can't afford it. You haven't gone on the record

> **SHOULD I BRING A SIGN?**
>
> Signs can be useful for reinforcing the sense of broad agreement with your message. However, if you're holding an oppositional sign, staffers will almost certainly not give you or the people with you the chance to get the mic or ask a question. If you have enough people to both ask questions and hold signs, though, then go for it!

   opposing this. Will you commit here and now to vote no on Bill X to cut Medicare?"

AT THE TOWN HALL

1. **Get there early, meet up, and get organized.** Meet outside or in the parking lot for a quick huddle before the event. Distribute the handout of questions, and encourage members to ask the questions on the sheet or something similar.

2. **Get seated and spread out.** Head into the venue a bit early to grab seats at the front half of the room, but do not all sit together. Sit by yourself or in groups of two, and spread out throughout the room. This will help reinforce the impression of broad consensus.

3. **Make your voices heard by asking good questions.** When the MoC opens the floor for questions, everyone in the group should put your hands up and keep them there. Look friendly or neutral so that staffers will call on you. When you're asking a question, remember the following guidelines:

   » **Stick with the prepared list of questions.** Don't be afraid to read it straight from the printout if you need to.

   » **Be polite but persistent, and demand real answers.** MoCs are very good at deflecting or dodging questions they don't want to answer. If the MoC dodges, ask a follow-up question. If they aren't giving you real answers, then call them out for it. Other group members around the room should amplify by either booing the MoC or applauding you.

   » **Don't give up the mic until you're satisfied with the answer.** If you've asked a hostile question, a staffer will often try to limit your ability to follow up by taking the microphone back immediately after you finish speaking. They can't do that if you keep a firm hold on the mic. No staffer in their right mind wants to look like they're physically intimidating a constituent, so they will back off. If they object, then say politely but loudly: "I'm not finished. The MoC is dodging my question. Why are you trying to stop me from following up?"

   » **Keep the pressure on.** After one member of the group finishes, everyone should raise their hands again. The next member of the group to be called on should move down the list of questions and ask the next one.

4. **Support the group and reinforce the message.** After one member of your group asks a question, everyone should applaud to show that the feeling is shared throughout the audience. Whenever someone from your group gets the mic, they should note that they're building on the previous questions — amplifying the fact that you're part of a broad group.

5. **Record everything!** Assign someone in the group to use their smart phone or video camera to record other advocates asking questions and the MoC's response. While written transcripts are nice, unfavorable exchanges caught on video can be devastating for MoCs. These clips can be shared through social media and picked up by local and national media.

AFTER THE TOWN HALL

1. **Reach out to media, during and after the town hall.** If there's media at the town hall, the people who asked questions should approach them afterwards and offer to

speak about their concerns. When the event is over, you should engage local reporters on Twitter or by email and offer to provide an in-person account of what happened, as well as the video footage you collected. Example Twitter outreach:

".@reporter I was at Rep. Smith's town hall in Springfield today. Large group asked about Medicare privatization. I have video & happy to chat."

-Note: It's important to make this a public tweet by including the period before the journalist's Twitter handle. Making this public will make the journalist more likely to respond to ensure they get the intel first.

Ensure that the members of your group who are directly affected by specific threats are the ones whose voices are elevated when you reach out to media.

2. **Share everything.** Post pictures, video, your own thoughts about the event, etc., to social media afterwards. Tag the MoC's office and encourage others to share widely.

OPPORTUNITY 2
OTHER LOCAL PUBLIC EVENTS

In addition to town halls, MoCs regularly attend public events for other purposes — parades, infrastructure groundbreakings, etc. Like town halls, these are opportunities to get face time with the MoCs and make sure they're hearing about your concerns, while simultaneously changing the news story that gets written.

Similar to Town Halls, but with some tweaks. To take advantage of this opportunity, you can follow most of the guidelines above for town halls (filming, etc.). However, because these events are not designed for constituent input, you will need to think creatively about how to make sure your presence and message comes through loud and clear.

Tactics for these events may be similar to more traditional protests, where you're trying to shift attention from the scheduled event to your own message.

1. **Optimize visibility.** Unlike in town halls, you want your presence as a group to be recognizable and attention-getting at this event. It may make sense to stick together as a group, wear relatively similar clothing / message shirts, and carry signs in order to be sure that your presence is noticeable.

2. **Be prepared to interrupt and insist on your right to be heard.** Since you won't get the mic at an event like this, you have to attract attention to yourself and your message. Agree beforehand with your group on a simple message focused on a current or upcoming issue. Coordinate with each other to chant this message during any public remarks that your MoC makes. This can be difficult and a bit uncomfortable. But it sends a powerful message to your MOC that they won't be able to get press for other events until they address your concerns.

3. **Identify, and try to speak with, reporters on the scene.** Be polite, friendly, and stick to your message. For example, "We're here to remind Congresswoman Sara that her constituents are opposed to Medicare cuts." You may want to research in advance which local reporters cover MoCs or relevant beats, so that you know who to be looking for.

4. **Hold organizational hosts accountable.** Often events such as these will be hosted by local businesses or non-partisan organizations — groups that don't want controversy or to alienate the community. Reach out to them directly to express your concern that they are giving a platform to pro-Trump authoritarianism, racism, and corruption. If they persist, use social media to express your disappointment. This will reduce the likelihood that these organizations will host the Trump-friendly MoC in the future. MoCs depend on invitations like these to build ties and raise their visibility — so this matters to them.

OPPORTUNITY 3
IN-OFFICE VISITS / SIT-INS

Every MoC has at least one district office, and many MoCs have several spread through their district or state. These are public offices, open for anybody to visit — you don't need an appointment. You can take advantage of this to stage a sort of impromptu town hall meeting by showing up with a small group. It is much harder for district or DC staff to turn away a group than a single constituent, even without an appointment.

1. **Find out where your MoCs local offices are.** The official webpage for your MoC will list the address of every local office. You can find those web pages easily through a simple Google search. In most cases, the URL for the a House member will be www.[lastname].house.gov, and the URL for Senate offices is www.[lastname].senate.gov.

2. **Plan a trip when the MoC is there.** Most MoC district offices are open only during regular business hours, 9am-5pm. While MoCs spend a fair amount of time in Washington, they are often "in district" on Mondays and Fridays, and there are weeks designated for MoCs to work in district. The MoC is most likely to be at the "main" office — the office in the largest city in the district, and where the MoC's District Director works. Ideally, plan a time when you and several other people can show up together.

3. **Prepare several questions ahead of time.** As with the town halls, you should prepare a list of questions ahead of time.

4. **Politely, but firmly, ask to meet with the MoC directly.** Staff will ask you to leave or at best "offer to take down your concerns." Don't settle for that. You want to speak with the MoC directly. If they are not in, ask when they will next be in. If the staffer doesn't know, tell them you will wait until they find out. Sit politely in the lobby. Note, on any given weekend, the MoC may or may not actually come to that district office.

5. **Note that office sit-ins can backfire**, so be very thoughtful about the optics of your visit. This tactic works best when you are protesting an issue that directly affects you and/or members of your group (e.g. seniors and caregivers on Medicare cuts, or Muslims and allies protesting a Muslim registry). Being polite and respectful throughout is critical.

6. **Meet with the staffer.** Even if you are able to get a one-off meeting with the MoC, you are most often going to be meeting with their staff. In district, the best person to meet with is the District Director, or the head of the local district office you're visiting. There are real advantages to building a relationship with these staff. In some cases, they may be more open to progressive ideas than the MoC him/herself, and having a good meeting with/building a relationship with a supportive staff member can be a good way to move your issue up the chain of command. Follow these steps for a good staff meeting:

- » Have a specific "ask" — E.g. vote against X, cosponsor Y, publicly state Z, etc.
- » Leave staff with a **brief** write up of your issue, with your ask clearly stated.
- » Share a personal story of how you or someone in your group is personally impacted by the specific issue (health care, immigration, medicare, etc.).
- » Be polite — Yelling at the underpaid, overworked staffer won't help your cause.
- » Be persistent — Get their business card and call/email them regularly; ask if the MoC has taken action on the issue.

7. **Advertise what you're doing.** Communicate on social media and with the local reporters you follow what is happening. Take and send pictures and videos with your group: "At Congresswoman Sara's office with 10 other constituents to talk to her about privatizing Medicare. She refuses to meet with us and staff won't tell us when she will come out. We're waiting."

OPPORTUNITY 4
MASS CALLS

Mass office calling is a light lift, but it can actually have an impact. Tea Partiers regularly flooded congressional offices with calls at opportune moments, and MoCs noticed.

1. **Find the phone numbers for your MoCs.** Again, you can find your local MoCs and their office phone numbers at www.callmycongress.com.

2. **Prepare a single question per call.** For in-person events, you want to prepare a host of questions, but for calls, you want to keep it simple. You and your group should all agree to call in on one specific issue that day. The question should be about a live issue — e.g. a vote that is coming up, a chance to take a stand, or some other time-sensitive opportunity. The next day or week, pick another issue, and call again on that.

3. **Find out who you're talking to.** In general, the staffer who answers the phone will be an intern, a staff assistant, or some other very junior staffer in the MoCs office. But you want to talk to the legislative staffer who covers the issue you're calling about. There are two ways to go about doing this:

   » Ask to speak to the staffer who handles the issue (immigration, health care etc). Junior staff are usually directed to not tell you who this is, and instead just take down your comment instead.

   » On a different day, call and ask whoever answers the phone, "Hi, can you confirm the name of the staffer who covers [immigration/health care/etc]?" Staff will generally tell you the name. Say "thanks!" and hang up. Ask for the staffer by name when you call back next time.

4. **If you're directed to voicemail, follow up with email.** Then follow up again. Getting more senior legislative staff on the phone is tough. The junior staffer will probably just tell you "I checked, and she's not at her desk right now, but would you like to leave a voicemail?" Go ahead and leave a voicemail, but don't expect a call back. Instead, after you leave that voicemail, follow up with an email to the staffer. If they still don't respond, follow up again. If they still don't respond, let the world know that the MoC's office is dodging you.

   Congressional emails are standardized, so even if the MoC's office won't divulge that information, you can probably guess it if you have the staffer's first and last name.

   » **Senate email addresses:** For the Senate, the formula is: StafferFirstName_StafferLastName@MoCLastName.senate.gov. For example, if Jane Doe works for Senator Roberts, her email address is likely "Jane_Doe@roberts.senate.gov"

   » **House email addresses:** For the House, the formula is simpler: StafferFirstName.StafferLastName@mail.house.gov. For example, if Jane Doe works in the House, her email address is likely "Jane.Doe@mail.house.gov"

5. **Keep a record of the conversation.** Take detailed notes on everything the staffer tells you. Direct quotes are great, and anything they tell you is public information that

can be shared widely. Compare notes with the rest of your group, and identify any conflicts in what they're telling constituents.

6. **Report back to media and your group.** Report back to both your media contacts and your group what the staffer said when you called.

SAMPLE CALL DIALOGUE

Staffer: Congresswoman Sara's office, how can I help you?

Caller: Hi there, I'm a constituent of Congresswoman Sara's. Can I please speak with the staffer who handles presidential appointments issues?

Staffer: I'm happy to take down any comments you may have. Can I ask for your name and address to verify you're in the Congresswoman's district?

Caller: Sure thing. [Gives name/address]. Can I ask who I'm speaking with?

Staffer: Yes, this is Jeremy Smith.

Caller: Thanks, Jeremy! I'm calling to ask what the Congresswoman is doing about the appointment of Steve Bannon to serve in the White House. Bannon is reported as saying he didn't want his children to go to a school with Jews. And he ran a website that promoted white nationalist views. I'm honestly scared that a known racist and anti-Semite will be working feet from the Oval Office. Can you tell me what Congresswoman Sara is going to do about it?

Staffer: Well I really appreciate you calling and sharing your thoughts! I of course can't speak for the Congresswoman because I'm just a Staff Assistant, but I can tell you that I'll pass your concerns on to her.

Caller: I appreciate that Jeremy, but I don't want you to just pass my concerns on. I would like to know what the Congresswoman is doing to stop this.

[If they stick with the "I'm just a staffer" line, ask them when a more senior staffer will get back to you with an answer to your question.]

Staffer: I'm afraid we don't take positions on personnel appointments.

Caller: Why not?

Staffer: Personnel appointments are the President's responsibility. We have no control over them.

Caller: But Congresswoman Sara has the ability to speak out and say that this is unacceptable. Other members of Congress have done so. Why isn't Congresswoman Sara doing that?

Staffer: As I said, this is the President's responsibility. It's not our business to have a position on who he chooses for his staff.

Caller: It is everyone's business if a man who promoted white supremacy is serving as an advisor to the President. The Congresswoman is my elected representative, and I expect her to speak out on this.

Staffer: I'll pass that on.

Caller: I find it unacceptable that the Congresswoman refuses to take a position. I'll be notifying my friends, family, and local newspaper that our Congresswoman doesn't think it's her job to represent us or actually respond to her constituents' concerns.

CONCLUSION

"Change will not come if we wait for some other person or some other time. We are the ones we've been waiting for. We are the change that we seek."
- President Barack Obama

We wrote this guide because we believe that the coming years will see an unprecedented movement of Americans rising up across the country to protect our values, our neighbors, and ourselves. Our goal is to provide practical understanding of how your Members of Congress (MoCs) think, and how you can demonstrate to them the depth and power of the opposition to Donald Trump and Republican congressional overreach. This is not a panacea, nor is it intended to stand alone. We strongly urge you to marry the strategy in this guide with a broader commitment to creating a more just society, building local power, and addressing systemic injustice and racism.

Finally, this guide is intended as a work in progress, one that we hope to continue updating as the resistance to the Trump agenda takes shape. We are happy to offer support to anybody interested in building on the tactics outlined in this guide, and we hope that if you find it useful or put any of the tactics described above into action, that you will let us know how it goes. Feel free to ping some of us on Twitter with questions, edits, recommendations, feedback/stories about what is helpful here, etc: @IndivisibleTeam, @ezralevin, @angelrafpadilla, @texpat, @Leahgreenb. Or email IndivisibleAgainstTrump@gmail.com.

Good luck — we will win.

Made in the USA
San Bernardino, CA
06 February 2017